WHOSE POO?

POO ON THE FARM

by
Emilie Dufresne

BEARPORT
PUBLISHING

Minneapolis, Minnesota

Credits:

All images are courtesy of Shutterstock.com, unless otherwise specified. With thanks to Getty Images, Thinkstock Photo, and iStockphoto.

Front Cover - Svietlieisha Olena, PremiumVector, Amanita Silvicora. Title typeface used throughout - PremiumVector. 2&4 - What's My Name. 4 - elbud, nlin.nee, Thanakorn Hongphan. 5 - MR.PRAWET THADTHIAM. 6&7 - NordStock. 7 - Eric Isselee, Tsekhmister. 8 - Aleksandra Saveljeva. 9 - siam sompunya, Viktorija Reuta. 10&11 - Olga_DigitalWork. 11 - Csanad Kiss, Eric Isselee, stockphoto mania. 12 - rtbilder. 13 - MyImages, Micha, Michele Paccione, curiosity. 14&15 - M Kun. 15 - Eric Isselee, Csanad Kiss, Tsekhmister. 16 - N-sky. 17 - O.PASH, Tiia Monto [CC BY-SA 3.0 (https://creativecommons.org/licenses/by-sa/3.0)], Studio Ayutaka, Jennifer Gottschalk. 18&19 - charnsitr. 19 - Eric Isselee, photomaster, yevgeniy11. 20 - Aneta Jungerova. 21 - MyImages - Micha, MSSA, Magicleaf. 22 - stockphoto mania, Kritsada.S. 23 - photomaster, viewsphotos.

Library of Congress Cataloging-in-Publication Data

Names: Dufresne, Emilie, author.
Title: Poo on the farm / Emilie Dufresne.
Description: Fusion. | Minneapolis, Minnesota : Bearport Publishing Company, [2021] | Series: Whose poo? | Includes bibliographical references and index.
Identifiers: LCCN 2020009368 (print) | LCCN 2020009369 (ebook) | ISBN 9781647473853 (library binding) | ISBN 9781647473907 (paperback) | ISBN 9781647473952 (ebook)
Subjects: LCSH: Animal droppings–Juvenile literature. | Farms–Juvenile literature.
Classification: LCC QL768 .D84 2020 (print) | LCC QL768 (ebook) | DDC 591.5–dc23
LC record available at https://lccn.loc.gov/2020009368
LC ebook record available at https://lccn.loc.gov/2020009369

For more information, write to Bearport Publishing, 5357 Penn Avenue South, Minneapolis, MN 55419. Printed in the United States of America.

CONTENTS

ALL ABOUT POO

Hard and round, squishy and soft, or runny and watery . . . poo comes in all different shapes and sizes.

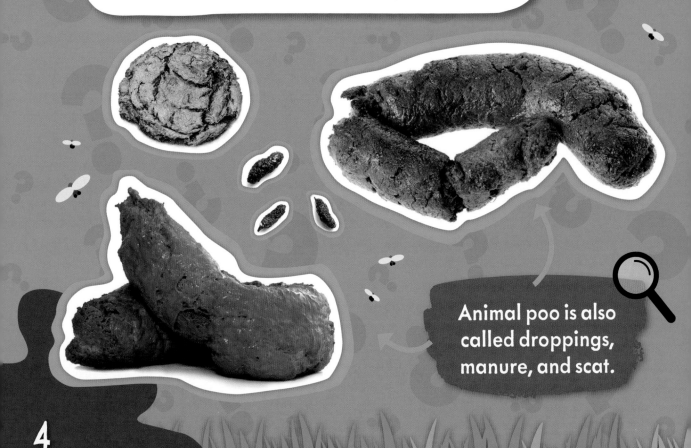

Animal poo is also called droppings, manure, and scat.

Don't touch any poo you find on the farm. Poo has lots of nasty things in it!

On the next pages, you will see poo on the farm. Read about the poo, and then think about which animal made it. Turn the page to see if you were right!

GIANT AND GRASSY

Wow—this is a big one! But whose poo is it?

Sniff, sniff! This poo doesn't smell too bad. The animal probably doesn't eat meat.

The poo is in ball shapes that have been squashed after dropping from high up.

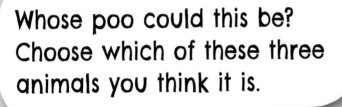

Whose poo could this be? Choose which of these three animals you think it is.

A big poo usually comes from a big animal.

There is a lot of grass and hay in this poo.

Don't look at me!

Pig

Horse

Faaaaarrt!

Do you really think I did that?

Sheep dog

7

WHOSE POO WAS IT?

It was the **horse's POO!**

It was me all along! I'm a big animal, and I make big poos!

A horse eats about 22 pounds (10 kg) of hay every day. That's like eating over 14 loaves of bread a day!

8

In a year, a horse can make almost 20,000 pounds (9 t) of poo. That's about the same weight as a *T. rex*!

Horses eat a lot, so they also poo a lot—about ten times every day!

Horses eat a lot of plants, which have many parts that can't be digested.

SPLATTERED AND FLAT

Watch your step—it's a wet one! But whose poo is it?

This poo is very wet and has the **texture** of oatmeal.

The pile is round and is about 1 inch (3 cm) high.

Whose poo could this be? Choose from these three animals.

It looks like it plopped on the ground from an animal that was standing up.

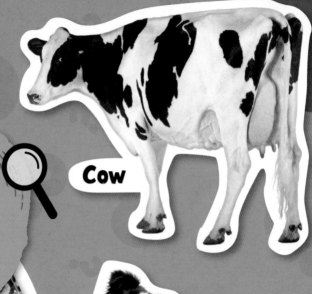

Cow

This poo is smooth with no large pieces of food in it.

Sheep dog

Chicken

Do you really think I could make that much?

WHOSE POO WAS IT?

It was the cow's POO!

All right, it was me! Now let me get back to eating. I have to graze for eight hours every day.

When a cow eats, it produces a lot of gas. The cow doesn't just fart—it burps as well!

BURP

12

Cows have to chew the cud, which means they throw up the food they have already eaten back into their mouths and chew it again. This makes it easier to digest.

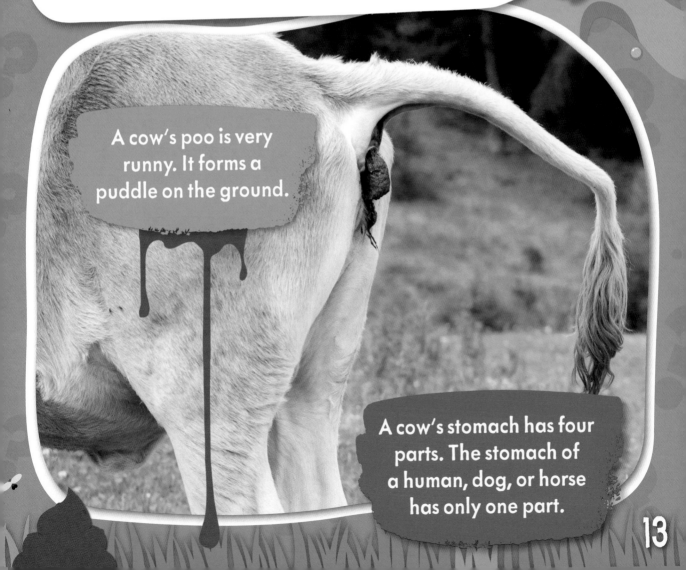

A cow's poo is very runny. It forms a puddle on the ground.

A cow's stomach has four parts. The stomach of a human, dog, or horse has only one part.

13

BUNCH OF BERRIES

What an odd shape! Whose poo could it be?

This poo looks like pebbles that have been squished together.

This poo is smooth without pieces of food in it.

14

Whose poo could this be? Choose from these three animals.

This animal probably grazes throughout the day.

There are lots of piles of this poo spread across the field.

Sheep

Pig

It doesn't smell like one of mine. . . .

Sheep dog

15

WHOSE POO WAS IT?

It was the **sheep's POO!**

Oh, was it me? I hadn't even noticed. I poo all the time.

Sheep chew the cud like cows do. This makes their poo smooth and uniform.

Sheep can poo and eat at the same time!

Don't try that at home!

Sheep stand up and walk around when they poo.

Sheep eat and poo throughout the day, so their droppings are everywhere.

17

FIRM AND FOUL

Plug your nose—it's a real stinker! But whose poo is it?

The poo has a long log shape and is chocolate-brown.

This poo smells really bad.

Whose poo could this be? Choose from these three animals.

There are clumps of grass and mud around this poo. This animal probably kicks and scrapes the ground after pooing.

The poo has the texture of wet clay.

Goat

Sheep dog

Even I think that stinks!

Pig

WHOSE POO WAS IT?

It was the **dog's** **POO!**

It was mine all along! I kicked up those pieces of grass and mud, too!

Dogs scrape and kick the ground with their back legs to fling mud and grass. This covers the poo and marks their territory.

Maybe one day I will be able to make a poo as big and as stinky as yours, Mommy!

Dogs eat a lot of meat. Meat makes their poo extra stinky.

Dog poo can also smell a lot if they eat processed food.

DOG FOOD

21

BONUS POO!

Chickens don't pee like humans do. Instead, their pee comes out with their poo. It is a white color!

Poo

Pee

22

POO-SPLOSION!

Farmers can have big problems with pig poo. If pig poo starts piling up, it can explode without warning!

A pig can make about 11 pounds (5 kg) of poo every day. That's 10 times as much as a human poos!

Look out . . . it's about to blow!

GLOSSARY

digested to have broken down food into things that can be used by the body

gas a thing that is like air, which spreads out to fill any space available

graze eat grass and other plants in a field

processed when food is treated in a way to make it last longer

territory the area where an animal lives and finds its food

texture the look or feel of something

uniform having the same size and shape throughout

INDEX